Hot and C

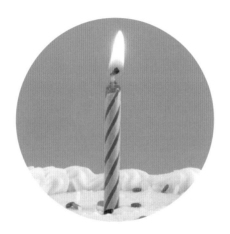

by Anne Giulieri

I see the sun.
It is hot.

I see the snow.
It is cold.

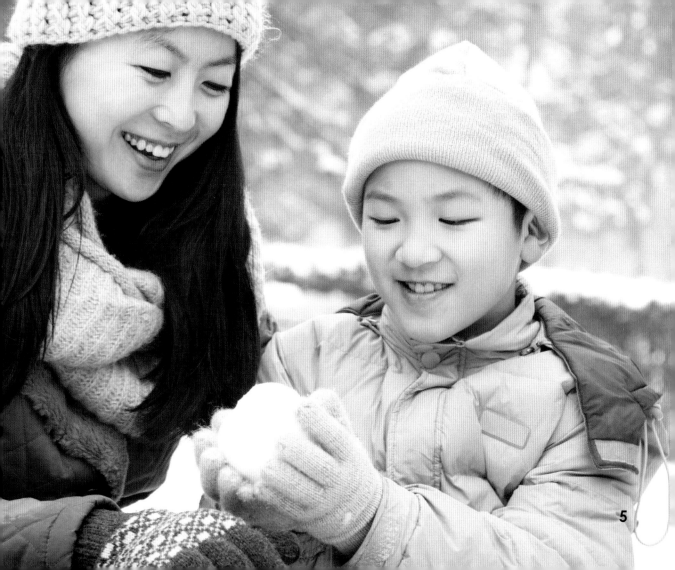

I see the fire.
It is hot.

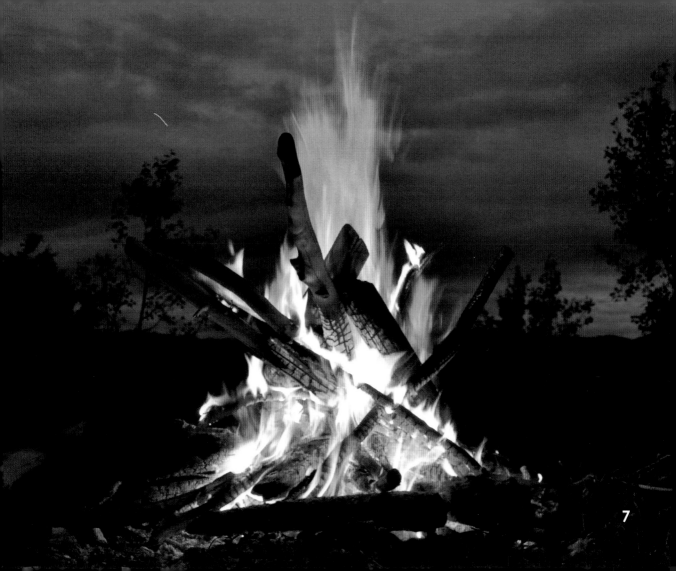

I see the ice.
It is cold.

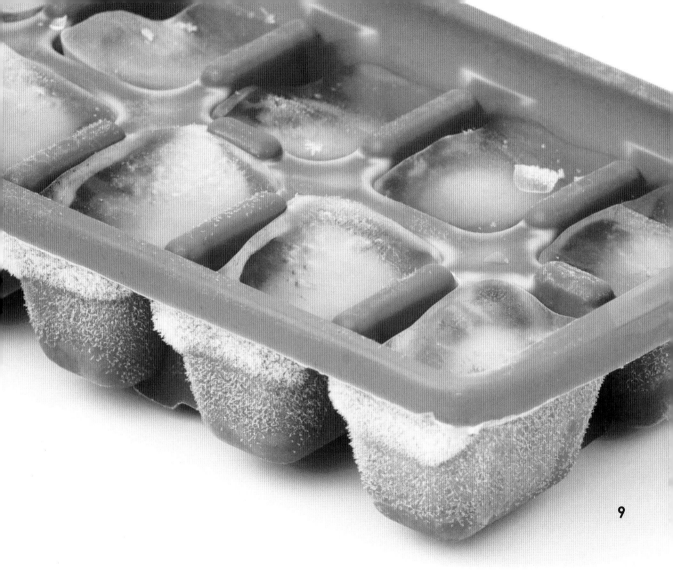

9

I see the pan.
It is hot.

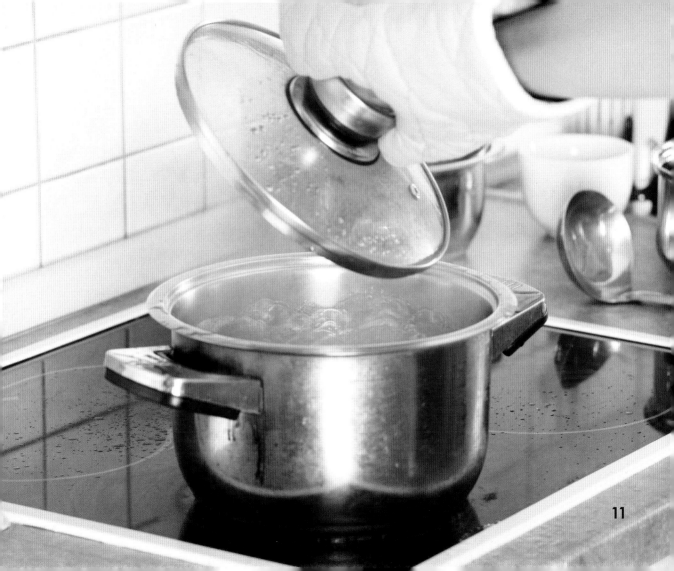

I see the milk.
It is cold.

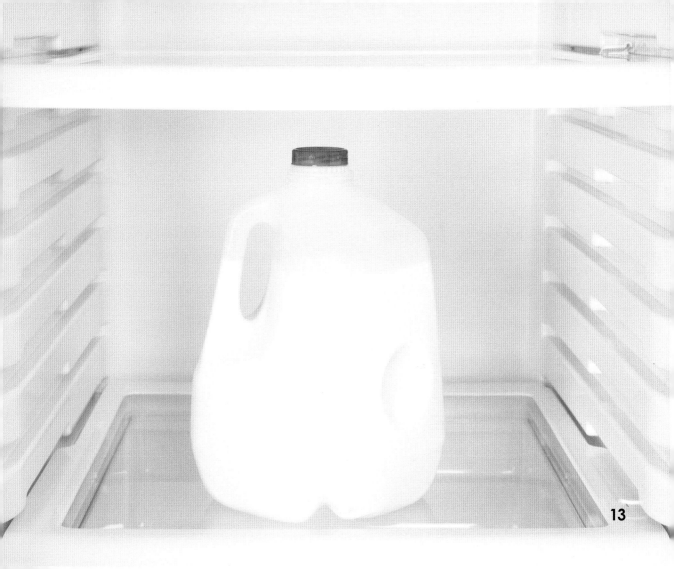

I see the candle.
It is hot.

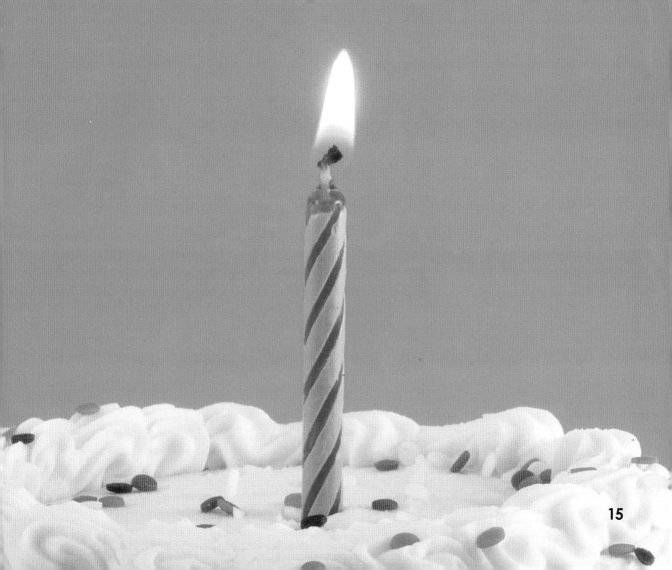

I see the ice cream.
It is cold.